A PARENT'S SURVIVAL GUIDE TO COLLEGE AND FINANCIAL AID

2ND EDITION

JIM TRIMBOLI

A Parent's Survival Guide to College and Financial Aid
2nd Edition
© James Trimboli 2016
ALL RIGHTS RESERVED

No part of this book may be reproduced or transmitted in any form or by any means, electronic or mechanical, including photocopying, recording or by any information retrieval system.

Also available in ebook format and through industry distribution channels. Booksellers and organizations may contact the publisher or author for bulk rate information.

Edited by Leslie Turner
leslie@encouragebooks.com

Published and distributed by:

Encourage Publishing, LLC
New Albany, Indiana
812.987.6148
info@encouragebooks.com
www.encouragebooks.com

ISBN 978-0-9962067-2-3

Distributed worldwide.

A PARENT'S SURVIVAL GUIDE TO COLLEGE AND FINANCIAL AID

2ND EDITION

Contents

	Foreword	4
	About the Author	5
	Introduction	7
Chapter 1	What to Consider When Choosing a College	9
Chapter 2	What is Financial Aid?	19
Chapter 3	How Is Student Need Determined?	31
Chapter 4	Types of Government Aid	35
Chapter 5	What Every Student and Parent Needs to Know about Student Loans	41
Chapter 6	Budgeting and Building Positive Credit	51
Chapter 7	Top Ten Most Costly Parent Mistakes	57
Chapter 8	Avoiding Scholarship Pitfalls	65
Chapter 9	Before Day One	75
Chapter 10	After Day One	79
	Endnotes	83
	Additional Resources	85

Foreword

Jim Trimboli's "A Parent's Survival Guide to College and Financial Aid" is a standout resource that gets to the heart of what students and their families need to know when facing two of life's most important decisions: choosing a college and financing a college education.

The book's clear and concise approach displays Trimboli's skill for making a complex process seem far less daunting, in fact, making it quite manageable. This book should be required reading for all families prior to beginning the college decision and financial aid process.

Patricia R. Thompson, Assistant Vice Chancellor
Student Financial Aid Services
State University of New York, System Administration

Dedication

This book is dedicated to my wife and three children,
my late mother who always encouraged me to write,
and the hard working people in the
financial aid industry.

About the Author

Jim Trimboli has been employed in the financial aid industry since 1999, serving as Director of Financial Aid for the State University of New York (SUNY) at Niagara County Community College, located in Sanborn, New York, since 2004. Beginning in 2015 Jim also serves as interim Admissions director at NCCC.

He holds a Master's Degree in Applied Economics from Buffalo State College as well as an Associate's Degree in Business Management from Bryant & Stratton Business College and a Bachelor's Degree in Business Resource Development from Medaille College. Jim is also a contributing author in the National Association of Student Financial Aid Administrators books "You're The Director: A Guide To Leadership in Student Financial Aid", 1st and 2nd Editions.

Jim presents regularly at national and regional higher education conferences and is a member of SUNY's Statewide Default Prevention Task Force and Financial Literacy Sub-Committee, which was responsible for statewide procurement that provided financial literacy for students and parents throughout the state of New York.

Jim is past chair of SUNY's Shared Services-Loan Verification Sub-Committee and is a regularly-featured speaker on Financial Wellness and Financial Literacy topics for incoming Niagara County Community College students and parents, local high schools, civic organizations, nationally recognized radio programs as well as other community-sponsored events.

Jim experienced a parent's pride and the perspective of helping a child through the college selection and financing process when his oldest son entered college in 2011, graduating in 2015. This experience, added to his many years of coaching youth ice hockey in his local community, gave Jim an understanding of the need and a heart for helping parents, as well as their children, through this precarious phase of life.

Jim lives in historic Lewiston, New York with his wife, Lisa, three children, James Jr., Kayley and Alex, and dog Daisy. When he's not speaking, coaching, or helping students and neighboring schools through his work, Jim enjoys fishing in the Lower Niagara River, spending time with his family and working on his six acres of land.

Introduction

Someone once said "Time is a great thief". Where does the time go? If you're like me it may seem like only yesterday when you brought your child home from the hospital; in a blink of an eye it's now time to send him or her off to college. Over the past eighteen years some of us may have set aside an entire college fund, others may have squirreled away what they could afford, and unfortunately others did not plan on this day arriving so suddenly. Whatever your financial situation may be, this book is sure to help you navigate the daunting task of helping your child fund their education.

I have spent almost twenty years of my life working in the financial aid industry. Twelve of those years I have been the Director of Financial Aid for a community college that serves over 8,000 students each year. Throughout my years in financial aid I have given countless words of advice to students and their families regarding their financial aid packages, conducted scores of financial aid presentations, and helped thousands of students and family members navigate the complicated financial aid process.

Most recently I have served as interim Admissions director, seeing first-hand the most common mistakes students and parents make in the admissions and college selection process, as well as the confusion new students experience in their first experience applying for college.

Oh, did I forget to mention that I am also the parent of a college graduate? Although the names of the folks I have helped have changed over the years, the look of consternation on the faces of families dealing with planning how to pay for college has not changed. Families and students today are faced with ever increasing tuition costs and decreasing resources to help offset these costs. The challenge for parents and students alike is to fund a quality education without incurring a heap of debt from which there is no escape.

This book contains information that will help you seamlessly navigate through the complicated financial aid process and give you some particular advice on how to keep college expenses down, help you and your student avoid expensive mistakes and learn easy tips to succeed in college.

My goal for you by the end of this book is to give you peace of mind through the process of funding your child's education and getting them through those first precarious steps of going to college.

Chapter 1

What to Consider When Choosing a College

(So Many Choices, So Little Time!)

What to study

Unfortunately, many students and their families wait until the last minute to decide on what college they want to attend and what course of study they wish to pursue. Parents and their children ideally should begin this conversation no later than the beginning of their son or daughter's junior year of high school. Some may argue that this is too late to begin this discussion; many parents might be pleasantly surprised to find that their child has already begun thinking about which course of study they want to undertake. Even if your child doesn't have a career or field of study in mind, at least you're taking the first steps in a long journey of trying to get your child to do some critical thinking about their future educational goals.

According to a survey conducted in 2006 by New York University's School of Continuing and Professional Studies, "a rarefied group, admittedly, but not necessarily atypical, expected, on average, to change careers three times in their lifetimes, and only 28 percent expected life long careers (1)". College Parents of America states that "It may help parents understand that most college students, some studies suggest a figure as high as 80%, change their major at least once (2)".

By reading the preceding two quotes a parent can reasonably deduct why it is so important to inquire early and often as to what your future college student has in mind. It is better that your child changes his or her mind before they enter a university when it costs nothing, than after they are committed to and enrolled in a field of study. Let's face it: did any of us really know what we wanted to do when we were eighteen years old? Many adults in their thirties and forties still struggle with the career or educational path they want to pursue.

What type of institution

There are many institutions of higher education in this country. There are public and private two year colleges, there are public and private four year universities, and there are technical, trade, business, and community colleges. If that is not enough for one to grasp, there are also graduate and post graduate colleges. To further complicate the issue of choice each one of these options has its own particular price tag.

Next to purchasing a home, a college education is quickly becoming the second largest investment a person can make in their lifetime. The key word is "investment". Unlike other big ticket items you will purchase in your lifetime, a college education is something no one can every take away from you; your degree will never wear out and cannot be traded in or given back. A college education, simply put, is a piece a paper that, coupled with hard work, desire, commitment and dedication, is a license to reach any level of potential in your career field, whether that be personal fulfillment, world-changing accomplishment or even unlimited income. It's not the piece of paper that will make or break your student; it's the dedication and effort they put into their degree and the connections they make along the way that will carry them.

Neither does a degree have to be from an Ivy-league or private school to have value. Many students, for example, who started at a community college and continued on at a public university now earn six figure incomes, thanks to hard work coupled with continued education. Though a solid K-12 education really does help you succeed in college, you may be the valedictorian of your high school with a full scholarship to Harvard and still end up a college drop out. Conversely, you could be an "average" student like most people and truly hit your stride in college. In the game of life there are no guarantees for college students. It's like the old saying "hard work beats talent when talent doesn't work hard". That's why it's so important for college students to make the right choices early on and be committed to their course of study.

Mr. Patrick Banard, high school track coach at Tonawanda High School in Erie County, New York, encouraged his teams with the reminder that the difference between being involved with something and committed to it is like ham and eggs. The chicken is involved while the pig is committed. You should instill that thought into your child throughout the college selection process and do your best to help her assess whether or not she is ready to commit herself fully to her education and to the course of study she selects.

Case Study: Parents talk "commitment"

My wife and I made too much for our child to qualify for any grants that look at financial need, but not enough to send him wherever he wanted to study. We were anxious to help him avoid unnecessary student loan debt, but we had financial limits. We compared college costs and examined our budget early in his senior year of high school.

We knew our son could succeed academically at any college he desired; however, if he chose the local community college we could afford my wife and I agreed we would pay his full tuition and fees, along with his books. If he decided to attend a different college, we would only pay up to the same amount we had already pledged to come up with for the community college and he would be on the hook for the rest of the other college's cost.

Since there is a limit to how much a student can borrow in a year, this meant certain college choices would be way out of his reach without some significant scholarships. To our amazement, before we could sit him down to have "the talk", our son had already figured out on his own it was more economically feasible for him to attend the community college. He made this choice for two reasons. First, he explained he chose the community college because of its program quality and, second, he told us that the community college was much cheaper.

He also informed us that along with the cheaper tuition he was able to dually enroll with a local four year university which offered him a $10,000 scholarship in his junior year to transfer to that institution. Once my wife and I picked ourselves off the floor we congratulated him on his wise decision and told him of our payment plan for tuition to offset his costs.

College or not?

It is also important to recognize that a traditional college education isn't for everyone; even a person well-suited for college must be ready for the challenge in order to succeed. Is your child ready? Are they going to the right college for the right reasons? If not, expect some heart-breaking set-backs. All students face obstacles in college; the students least likely to push through those moments often already have one foot out the door because their heart isn't in it. Those same students may point to famously successful college drop-outs like Steve Jobs or Rush Limbaugh as evidence to support a decision to leave college. We can all recognize that these examples are the exception, not the rule, even for the most brilliant students. College is still the best path for long-term career growth and financial stability overall.

However, there are plenty of successful people that work in fields that do not require a college degree, such as the many skilled trade professions. They live productive and happy lives and are gainfully employed. Throughout my higher education career I have seen many parents pressure their children into going to college even though they show no interest or are just not ready. Please don't be "that parent". Though some students do need some strong encouragement, don't push your child toward college, or toward a particular college, for any of the following reasons:

1. He would be the first one in the family to go to college (or fulfill your own dream of a college education)

2. She would graduate from the same school you did, or enter the same profession

3. You want to impress someone else, maintain your family status, or are comparing your child to another student.

These are all roads to disaster. Just because the Joneses sent their cherub to an Ivy League college doesn't mean that your child is ready or wants to go to college. Forcing someone to go to college only leads to failure and an expensive waste of time and money, not to mention the damage it does to your relationship. Further, returning to college at a future date becomes significantly less likely because the first experience was negative.

Instead, set boundaries on how much support you are willing to give them if they choose *not* to continue their education. A conversation may go something like this: "Johnny, we are willing to sacrifice and stretch our living expenses a few more years to help you succeed in further education, but if you are ready to begin your work life instead, you are ready to begin living on your own." This dose of reality often helps them evaluate their life goals more easily.

What we can afford

When selecting a college you want to put all options on the table and evaluate them carefully. The first thing a family must decide on is the cost and how much they can afford out of their household budget. The amount you as a parent are willing to invest should be in balance with your child's commitment to succeed in college and with your own resources. Be careful not to overcommit or make promises you may later regret.

The previous case study illustrates you should not underestimate the value of your local community college or a four year public institution for a low- priced quality education. As compared to a private institution, public venues of higher education offer a similar product at reasonable prices. When I decided to go back for my Master's in economics later in life, I, too, was faced with a choice. Do I go back to my private pricey college which provided a quality education for my undergraduate degree, or do I go to a public institution that had a similar offering at a cheaper price?

Once I thought about the student loan debt that piled up on me and how it took me eight years to pay it off for my undergraduate work, I decided to give the public institution a shot. It proved to be one of the best decisions I ever made. Not only did I do very well in a tough program, my classes were small and, best of all, I was able to pay for my classes out of pocket rather than amass a pile of student loan debt that would have taken me several years to pay off.

When making the tough choice between sending your child to a public or private college please keep in mind it's not the college that Junior attends that matters as much as it is what your child does while he or she is there. Especially if your child is undecided about declaring a major, it may more advantageous for you to send them to a public college rather than private school in the long run. If your child changes their mind on a course of study it won't end up costing you a small fortune in the end.

Living arrangements

Before your child decides on an institution of higher education, they must consider living arrangements. In cases where the college is out-of-state, know the rules for incoming freshmen. Are they required to live on campus? Are you lucky enough to have a willing relative who lives in the area who will provide room and board for your child while they attend college? If they are required to live on campus, is a meal plan required? Make a list of furniture and everything else that your child will need to have while they are away from home. When all is said and done this can lead to an expensive bill on top of the cost of tuition.

Even though living allowances and room and board are considered in most colleges' financial aid packages, it could still add up to be a pretty hefty sum that will require an action plan on your part to decipher a way to fund this amount. If your child is planning to attend a college close to home it might be cheaper for you to help them buy a quality used car or let them take public transportation to commute back and forth to school rather than living on a local campus.

I have heard many parents talk about how they want the college dorm experience for their child at a local campus. This idea must be considered very carefully. Do you really want to encourage your child to take on extra debt so that they can find out what it is like living with several other people they don't know in a dorm room at a local college? Do you want this for them because you never had the opportunity? Or, are you anxious for them to move out for other reasons? Whatever your answer is, you must consider the financial ramifications that come with such a plan.

Books and supplies

The last significant college expense for your child is books and supplies. Once again, most campuses include book and supply allowances in their financial aid budgets; however, these items can add up quickly. When purchasing books and supplies, be a savvy consumer, just as you are with everything else you buy. With just a little forethought you can save your student a pile of money. For instance, many college bookstores sell used books at about half the price of a new book. Just like other stores, the supply of used books is limited; buy these books early before they are all snapped up.

After grades post and they know they don't need to repeat the class, your student may be able to return the textbook to the bookstore for a small credit, or list their books on a student textbook website to sell them for higher profit. Online websites are often great places to save a lot of money, but beware – returns may be tricky. Many bookstores now offer the wonderful option of renting books. The student simply signs an agreement with the bookstore promising to return the book in good condition at the end of the semester, leaving a deposit on a credit card to ensure that the book is brought back in good condition. The bookstore will often e-mail the student a reminder a few days before the book is to be returned. The best part of renting is that the student pays much less than if they purchased books.

Many colleges offer PDF versions of textbooks that can be read online, downloaded to a device or printed on demand at the student's cost, allowing the student to be selective about which pages they want to print. More and more colleges are able to offer ebook versions downloadable to a mobile device or computer; however, not all students study well with electronic versions. Don't feel you must invest in a tablet or laptop for your student; though it may be a good study tool you may not be able to afford it and there is usually a print version available also. If you decide to get an e-reader device, consider buying one without all the extras needed for gaming, a major distraction for college students.

Bookstores should always show all the versions they have available, and some colleges require students to purchase books from their bookstore. Keep receipts and know the return policy and deadline. Although I don't highly recommend this option, students can also wait until the start of classes to see if the instructor is actually going to use the book. Usually this information is found in the instructor's syllabus. If they are able to contact the instructor beforehand, students may want to inquire if the book listed will be required for that particular professor's class. Nothing used to aggravate me more in college then spending a hundred dollars or more on a book and then finding out the first day of class that the instructor decided he or she will not be using the text.

Computers, digital devices and software are considered legitimate school expenses, within reason. Your student may also be taking a class with high material or lab costs, such as an art class, field study or study abroad program. The student may be able to find extra funds for these unusually high expenses through the financial aid office by asking for a budget increase.

Chapter 2
What is Financial Aid?

When I speak to large groups of students and their parents, I often ask this question, "Is financial aid a privilege or an entitlement"? In other words, is it your right to receive financial aid? The first year, if you follow all of the steps and are eligible for a Pell grant, yes; that Pell grant is considered an "entitlement". However, ask any student who is not eligible to apply for financial aid, or who lost their eligibility, and you will learn quickly: receiving financial aid, even student loans, to help pay for college is a privilege, and a student could lose that privilege at any time.

A student can have their aid revoked for many unfortunate situations stemming from poor grades to non-attendance. That's why it is so important that students and parents have a full understanding of what financial aid is and how it works.

Financial aid, in a nutshell, includes any funds that help offset the educational costs for a student who is attending college. Some financial aid is based on need. Other types of financial aid are awarded based on other criteria such as grades. Financial aid can come from several sources which include but are not limited to the following: federal government sources (also known as "Title IV" funds), state sources, college sources (also known as institutional aid) and private sources. Within these sources are specific categories that most financial aid falls into which includes grants and scholarships ("free" money), work-study, and loans. Before we get into a description of each specific category of financial aid it is important to know how the federal government defines "need" and how financial need is determined.

Applying for aid – the FAFSA

In order to apply for federal (Title IV funds) and most state financial aid each student must complete a federal government form known as a Free Application for Federal Student Aid or FAFSA. The key word in this title is "free". Please be warned that there are many websites or agencies out there that will charge you to complete this form. Though some parents are happy to pay someone to do this and have the money to do so, for most families this is an unnecessary expense. Some students and their families end up, unfortunately, spending sometimes over a thousand dollars for something they could have done for themselves totally free of charge, often in as little as fifteen minutes. Don't fall into this trap. Applying for the FAFSA is easy and it's FREE.

In fact, it's a lot easier now than when many of today's parents went to college. Today most FAFSA forms are filed electronically; once you submit your FAFSA you receive an instant federal aid estimate and will have an answer on the amount of federal financial aid you qualify for sent to your email account within 1-3 business days.

All you will need is the following free government website to apply for and submit your FAFSA application to the federal government: **www.fafsa.gov**. At the end of the application, both the student and one parent, if the parent's information is required on the FAFSA, will be required to electronically sign the FAFSA through a secure password you will create through the website and use every year at www.fafsa.gov and other federal financial aid websites.

> ### Director's Tip:
> I always tell students and their families before they start the electronic FAFSA application to think of this process like a family project. First, gather the documentation you will need to complete the FAFSA application. Students will need their Social Security number, alien registration number(if you are not a U.S. citizen), driver's license, W-2 forms and federal income tax returns, bank statements, and any other annual benefit statements from the previous two years. Remember, for your son or daughter who is under the age of 24 these documents may also be required for parents.

Parent information on the FAFSA

One of the most frequent questions heard in a financial aid office is, "why do I have to include my parents' information? They are not going to be paying for my education!" Students who are considered "dependent" by the criteria on the FAFSA have to include parent information regardless of whether the parent is paying for their education or supporting the student in any way whatsoever; also, it does not matter whether or not the parent claims the student on their tax return, a common and costly misconception.

A dependent student as defined by the Federal Government FAFSA is a student that is under the age of **24** and does NOT meet any of the following criteria for independence:

CRITERIA FOR FILING AS AN INDEPENDENT STUDENT

1. The student is married.

2. The student is currently working on a master's or doctorate program.

3. The student is currently serving on active duty in the U.S. Armed Forces for purposes other than training or is a veteran.

4. The student has children _for whom they provide more than half of their support_ during the upcoming financial aid year.

5. The student has dependents (other than children or spouse) that live with _and receive more than have of their support from the student_.

6. On or after the student's 13th birthday, both parents were deceased or the student was in foster care or a dependent or ward of the court.

7. The student was considered an emancipated _minor_, as determined by a court in their state of legal residence.

8. The student was under court-ordered legal guardianship, as determined by the court in their state of legal residence.

9. At any time on or after July 1 of the current tax year for FAFSA purposes the student was determined to be an unaccompanied youth who was homeless or self-supporting and at risk of being homeless by:

    - Their high school or school district homeless liaison,

    - The director of an emergency shelter or transitional housing program funded by the U.S. Department of Housing and Urban Development, or

    - The director of a runaway youth basic center or transitional living program

If a dependent student meets any one of these conditions, the student can file as an independent student. What this means for mom or dad is that they do not have to provide any of their information on the FAFSA, nor do they have to sign it. Their child will be using only their own information to complete the FAFSA and only have to provide their own income information unless they were married, in which case their spouse's income and information would have to be included as well.

If a student who is under the age of 24 claims to qualify to be independent under the above criteria, that student may be required to bring documentation to the financial aid office that supports this claim. Examples of documents that may be required for submission by the financial office include but are not limited to: death certificates, marriage certificates, proof of emancipation or legal guardianship, military DD214 forms, IRS transcripts, and letters on high school or agencies' letterheads.

Please keep in mind that the financial aid office only asks for these documents when required to do so by the federal government. The financial aid office is only a conduit between the student and the federal government. Remember, it's the federal government's money; it doesn't belong to the student, the parent or the school, so whatever the federal government requires, the financial aid office must receive. Put simply, you will not receive your aid package until you comply with the government's requests.

One example of documentation that is often a source of contention with students is when a student who is under age 24 has a child or children of their own. In a case like this the student has to be able to prove that they support themselves and provide more than 50% of their children's support. A student in this scenario must have enough income to support their children and be using it for that purpose and for their own living expenses.

> ### Case Study: Students under age 24 with children
> Let's look at 21-year old Jessica and her daughter, Claire. Jessica and Claire live rent-free in a separate apartment in her parents' basement. Jessica works part-time and only earns about $2000 per year. Claire receives healthcare benefits through a county agency. When completing the FAFSA, Jessica's parents' information would be required; both Jessica and Claire would be included in the number in the household as well as the parents and any other members of their household.
>
> What if Jessica and Claire moved in with Claire's father, Gabe? Jessica and Gabe must both declare income even though they are not married, regardless of Jessica's age. Jessica would not include her parents' information on the FAFSA.
>
> If Jessica and Gabe get married, Jessica's parent information will also not be required on the following year's FAFSA, but Gabe's information will be required, even if he is not Claire's biological or adoptive father. Jessica and Gabe could file a special circumstance appeal for change in marital status through the office of financial aid if they marry during the school year, but this does not always guarantee more grant funding.*
> * For same-sex couples, same rules apply. Ask your financial aid office if you have questions.

The best rule of thumb when it comes to questions about whether a student under the age of 24 can be considered as an independent student is to speak with a qualified financial aid officer at the school the student plans to attend. In some circumstances, a student who would otherwise have to include parent information and get their signature may qualify for a dependency appeal if there are unique circumstances preventing them from getting parents' help.

FAFSA deadlines and details

When should the FAFSA be completed? FAFSA applications for the upcoming academic year will be available online as early as

October 1. Every state has its own deadline for students to qualify for state aid and there is a "Deadlines" link at www.fafsa.gov where you may look up the filing deadline for your own state.

State deadlines usually only matter if the student plans to attend college in the state where they, and their parents, legally reside; however, some colleges may use the state deadline for their own scholarship deadline. Review your college's website or contact the financial aid office to see if they have an earlier FAFSA filing deadline or require an additional application to be considered for other scholarships. Ideally, to allow a college proper time to process your student aid package and FAFSA, every student should try to complete the FAFSA as early as possible but no later than the state deadline.

> **Director's Tip:**
> Don't delay filing the FAFSA because your taxes aren't done. Beginning with the 2017/2018 school year, FAFSA looks at tax returns from two years back, which would have been filed by the previous April 15 unless you filed an extension. You should be able to import the correct tax information straight from the IRS website. It's fast, easy, and significantly reduces the chances you'll have to go through a sometimes lengthy process called "verification". If you did file an extension, you can use estimates and import corrected information soon after you file.

Missed the deadline? A student and their family can complete the FAFSA long after classes have begun and after stated deadlines and may still receive federal aid for those classes, provided the academic term has not ended. However please keep in mind that all FAFSA applications from students across the nation are processed by the Department of Education in the order that they are received and shared only with colleges the student lists on the FAFSA.

Colleges often receive a high volume of FAFSA data in late spring through late summer which slows their response time, especially if the student is required to submit additional paperwork. The longer a student waits to the send the application in, the longer the wait will be to receive an answer back on how much aid you may receive. If you want your aid ready before classes begin, file the FAFSA and complete any additional paperwork before your school's priority deadline. Remember to read all email correspondence. You may believe you have made all the deadlines but still have not received a financial aid award letter or admission letter.

This brings me to perhaps my most important advice, which can be summed up in one word: DILIGENCE.

Here's how students can be diligent:

- **Apply early.** Submit both your admissions applications and financial aid applications as early as possible to your top 3-5 school choices, even if you plan to retake your ACT or SAT.

- **Pay attention to detail.** Double-check your form entries and don't assume anything. Ask questions.

- **Follow up.** Check ALL emails, including your junk mail folder, and if you haven't received anything from the college don't assume everything is fine. Did someone else help you with your application? They may have used their own email. Ask them to check. Let's make it easy: read the lists on the next page and flag the page to check them again in the middle of the process.

> **Director's Tip:**
> Some colleges do not require the Social Security Number (SSN) on the Admissions application, but if students file the FAFSA they must also correctly enter their SSN on their ADMISSIONS application so the two records can match up.

Top FIVE Admissions Afflictions

(Or "why you haven't gotten your admissions letter")

1. You never applied (or just recently applied) for admission
2. There is a hold on your admission application*
3. You never asked your high school to send your transcript
4. You never took the placement test or remedial courses
5. You never had your SAT or ACT scores sent to the school

*Admissions applications can be held for many reasons, including completing the immunization acknowledgement. You don't need to get a shot (though it may be wise) - just read and acknowledge. Check with Admissions. They are busy, so if you don't get an email response, call in.

Top FIVE FAFSA Fails

(Or "why you haven't gotten your financial aid letter")

1. You selected the wrong school code or academic year on the FAFSA or forgot to include that school code.
2. You were picked for verification and never responded to the college's requests for this required information.
3. Your FAFSA was rejected OR you never clicked the "Submit" button*
4. You put the wrong certificate, degree, or grade level on the FAFSA.
5. You have an admission problem! (See "Admissions Afflictions")

*A couple days after filing, log in to www.fafsa.gov and check your FAFSA status. If you have a missing signature, an incorrect Social Security Number, never clicked "submit" or have some other issue you can correct it.

> **Director's Tip:**
> It usually takes up to two weeks for schools to receive, process and respond to FAFSA records, and Admissions applications are processed even more quickly. If the student has not received a communication within that time frame, they should contact the office and be persistent. Students: if an email doesn't get a response, call in. Always include your student ID or have it handy.
>
> Parents, remember: schools often cannot take calls from the parents about these issues, unless the solution requires parent information or action. Your student should initiate all calls and emails. This has to do with privacy laws (FERPA - Family Education Right to Privacy Act) and will frustrate you, but - it's the law.

I have already mentioned that the FAFSA stands for Free Application for Student Aid. You are applying for grant and loan money from the U. S. Department of Education using this form, and states and colleges also use it for this purpose. Grant money available under the FAFSA includes the Pell Grant, Supplemental Educational Opportunity Grant (SEOG), the TEACH grant and the Work Study award. I will discuss these in full detail in the next chapter.

Basically, the Pell and SEOG grants are "free" money for a student to put toward offsetting the cost of attending college. Though all federal grants and loans are awarded from the government based on household income and need, the neediest students (low income students) as deemed by the federal government are awarded these two particular types of grants.

Often students will say to me that they don't fill out the FAFSA because their parents make too much money. I remind these students that if they wish to apply for a low-interest federal student loan they are required to fill out the FAFSA. Federal government Title IV regulations allow students to borrow a limited amount of low interest student loans every year without a credit check. Some colleges also require the student to fill out the FAFSA application in order to apply for scholarships. Also, family income could change, making you eligible for an appeal.

Need help completing the FAFSA? Students and families needing help to complete their FAFSA can find dates and times online at **www.collegegoalsundayusa.org** of free events held throughout their state and staffed by financial aid professionals, just to help families complete the FAFSA. You may also call 800-433-3243 for short-answer assistance or visit your first-choice school's financial aid office.

More about the IRS Data Retrieval Tool

The Department of Education and the Internal Revenue Service created the process referred to as the IRS data retrieval tool, embedded in the electronic FAFSA application, to simplify the filing process. Using the tool is not required if you prefer to enter the information by hand.

In most cases, using the IRS data retrieval tool will not only make completing the electronic FAFSA faster and easier, it also may help students avoid a lengthy verification process which could require the student to bring additional documents into the financial aid office in order to receive their financial aid package. However, you may not be able to use the retrieval feature. If a parent remarried but did not file jointly with their new spouse, they cannot use the retrieval tool. If they were divorced or widowed after filing jointly, they also cannot use the retrieval tool. Getting help from the financial aid office is probably best in these scenarios.

Additional verification can often be avoided by double-checking form entry errors on the electronic FAFSA before signing and submitting the FAFSA. Just because you receive an initial confirmation that your FAFSA application was received doesn't mean you are home free. Some common errors are:

- Incorrect Social Security Numbers
- Marital status incorrectly stated (use most recent)
- Parent/stepparent income excluded
- Untaxed income or assets excluded or overstated
- U.S. income taxes paid taken from the W2 instead of the tax return
- Household size/number in college is too low or too high
- Real estate and investment net worth misstated

Students and their parents, remember: there are companies and websites that will file FAFSA forms for a fee. You can file this form yourself at no cost. FAFSA is short for **FREE** Application for Federal Student Aid.

> **Director's Tip:**
> Has parent or student income dropped in the past year, or are changes coming? Go ahead and do the tax return import as prompted, then call or check the website of the financial aid office where your student will attend to see if they have a special circumstance appeal process. Changes in marital status, job loss, high medical bills and family size increase are just a few examples of possible adjustments only the financial aid office may make.

Chapter 3
How Is Student Need Determined?

Now that you have helped your student submit their FAFSA, you're probably wondering about the next steps.

The financial data that a student submits on their FAFSA is then processed by the Department of Education via something called a "needs methodology formula" (6), which is a fairly complicated algorithim used by the federal government to calculate the expected family contribution and estimate the student's financial aid eligibility. This formula uses dozens of weighted factors to evaluate and set a baseline for the family's ability to pay for educational costs.

Financial aid is a limited resource so, in essence, this formula determines who the neediest of students are based on household size, income, certain assets and many, many other factors. The formula that the federal government uses to determine need is:

Cost of Attendance (COA)

- Expected Family Contribution (EFC)

= Financial Need

In order to understand how this formula works, we must break down each component of this formula to gain an understanding of exactly what the government is looking at to determine what goes into the cost of a student going to college and what items are consisered by the government to offset what a family is expected to pay for their son or daughter to attend an institution of higher education. The cost of attendance to a college includes the following:

- Tuition and fees
- Room and board
- Books and supplies
- Transportation
- Miscellaneous personal expenses

COA may also be increased to include:

- Loan fees
- Study abroad costs
- Dependent care and dependent tuition expenses
- Expenses related to a disability
- Purchase of education-related technology

All of the previous expenses are what a college calculates to be in a student's budget for the year. In essence, the college's COA considers what the typical student's expected expenses will be from various sources within the academic year. The COA is just an estimate and is not a good indicator of the actual bill. It is used to establish a maximum amount of aid any one student may receive during one year of college, but also does not imply the student will receive that much aid.

The second part of this formula examines the student's expected family contribution, or EFC for short. All sources of a student's family income and assets that were reported on their FAFSA are examined in this process. This formula also looks at your household family size and how many family members are in college or a career school. The lower the family household income and the greater the number of family members in college, the higher a family's need for financial aid is.

Please also note that the EFC will stay the same regardless of the college selected. In a nutshell, the EFC is all about what the government deems is a fair amount that the family should be able to provide that year in order to help cover the cost of the student's education. Families are never required to pay a student's bill, and including parent information on the FAFSA in no way obligates the parent to pay for the student's education. This is a common fear among parents. Only the student is responsible for the cost of their education.

The EFC also does not necessarily represent the amount a student will literally have to pay the school and does not mean the government will be able to cover the rest of the bill. In most cases, families are already providing room and board, transportation and personal expenses, for example, and the student would have to pay the school only the amount of the bill not covered by the student's financial aid. Still, it stands to reason that a school with a higher COA is going to have a higher bill to pay as well, and a family with a low EFC is going to have more financial aid available to help offset that bill.

The chart that follows illustrates how the needs formula could impact a student's cost of attending college.

Examples of EFC and Need

	College A	*College B*	*College C*
COA	$5,500	$30,000	$60,000
minus EFC	- $5,000	- $5,000	- $5,000
Financial need	$500	$25,000	$55,000

Creating your own chart like this can be useful as a guide to help a parent and a student navigate through college expense and their personal finances in order to come up with a game plan to help offset the expense of going to college. It will also help students and their families determine which colleges are affordable options and which institutions of higher education may be out of their financial reach.

Chapter 4
Types of Government Aid

This chapter will cover the types of federal and state financial aid that are available and the criteria that make a student and their families eligible for grants and student loans. Please remember that it is a government requirement that a student and their family complete the FAFSA in order to begin the process of qualifying for these federal and state aid programs. Some states may have additional filing requirements.

Pell Grant

The Pell Grant is named after former Rhode Island Senator Claiborne Pell, who sponsored a bill helping fund low and moderate income students so they could attend college (7)". The Pell grant, like any other grant fund, is "free" money based on household income and assets that a student does not have to pay back.* The Pell Grant award amount is based on COA, EFC and enrollment status. A student must be registered in a degree or certificate program and be enrolled in at least one class. The student must also maintain good academic standing according to their school's criteria in order to receive the award again.

Once the student receives a bachelor's degree or receives the equivalent of six years of Pell payments they are no longer eligible to receive the Pell Grant. To see the most recent annual Pell grant award for students attending full-time, visit www.studentaid.ed.gov.

*A student will have to repay all or part of their Pell grant received in the current academic term if their award was based on a class they never attended or if they stopped attending all classes early in the term.

> **Director's Tip:**
> Many first-year students are under the misconception that if they qualify for a Pell grant all of their expenses will be covered, including housing. Since the amount of Pell grant a student receives does not vary school by school, this cannot be true; in most cases a full Pell grant will not even be enough to cover all of the basic tuition, fees and books, except perhaps at some public community colleges. This is why it is so important to know the costs up front.

FSEOG Grant

FSEOG stands for the "Supplemental Educational Opportunity Grant". This grant is awarded first to those students with exceptional financial need who have the lowest EFCs at their institutions. Priority in awarding this grant is also given to students that are Pell eligible. To see the most current maximum annual FSEOG grant award visit www.studentaid.ed.gov.

Please note that the FSEOG is known as a campus-based program. This means that the campus you are attending has to participate and apply for this type of aid every year, and the award amount and criteria vary by school. The amount of FSEOG that each campus receives from the federal government is limited and can vary from year to year. Consequently, schools often run out of these funds in any given year. This is why it is important that you apply for your FAFSA early so you can ensure your award of FSEOG if you qualify.

Federal Work Study

Federal Work Study is also considered a campus-based program, so, once again, it is essential with this program that you submit the FAFSA as early as possible, since funds can be limited. The student does not necessarily have to be eligible for a Pell grant to receive this award. The Federal Work Study program allows students to be employed on or off campus with part-time jobs. Students receive a regular paycheck for hours worked during the academic year, up to the total of their work study award amount. This program is offered to both undergraduate and graduate students.

Personally I can't think of a better type of employment for a student for a plethora of reasons. First, work study is a very good way for a student to gain valuable work experience in higher education. A student can gain real life experiences working in various offices on campus. Another good reason to pursue a work study position is convenience. Students in many cases can work the hours they want and may want to fill in free time between classes. Students who work on campus also don't have to worry about the costs of transportation to and from work or about an employer requiring them to work during class time. Off-campus jobs in the student's field of study may also be available.

Please keep in mind that work study payments cannot generally be deducted from a tuition bill and must be paid in form of a salary though, in some schools, the bursar may be able to withhold payment at the student's request and apply it to the student's bill.

This is regular income that would be included on the student's tax return if they file. An added benefit of work-study is that income earned through work-study and declared as such on the FAFSA will not be included in the formula used to determine the student's EFC for the following year. one question asks how much of the student's declared income came from work-study. That amount is then deducted during the calculation.

TEACH Grant

The TEACH Grant is a relatively new grant program first offered by the U. S. Department of Education in 2007. TEACH stands for Teacher Education Assistance for College and Higher Education. In short, the TEACH Grant can provide free money up to $4,000 per year to students who plan to pursue a curriculum in the teaching profession. The savvy student should be aware that, upon applying for the TEACH Grant, he or she must sign a TEACH Grant contract which requires the student to serve and teach students in a high needs field for a least four academic years, within eight years of graduation or ceasing enrollment in the course of study as required by the grant.

All students thinking about applying for the TEACH Grant should fully understand that failure to complete all stipulations and requirements of the TEACH Grant will result in all TEACH Grant funds received under this program being converted to a Direct Unsubsidized Student Loan. For this reason, students and their families need to be prudent and ask the financial aid office at the college where they are attending for a copy of the regulations regarding the Teach Grant so students and their families can review these very carefully before obligating themselves to the grant. Please note that not all colleges offer the TEACH Grant so check with your financial aid office for availability.

Loans

Federal student loans will be available to any student attending at least 1/2 time and officially enrolled in a degree or certificate program. The student must have a current FAFSA on file, be in good academic standing and not be in default on any previous federal student loans. There is no credit check for federal student loans, however parent PLUS loans and private or alternative loan decisions will be based on credit standing. Federal student loans have lifetime and annual limits as well as caps based on class rank. Interest rates and terms are changeable and based on congressional action. The most current information on caps, limits, rates and terms can be found at www.studentloans.gov. The next chapter is a must-read for anyone looking into borrowing through the student loan program.

> **Director's Tip:**
> Parents, don't be tempted to promise your student you will pay off their student loans once they graduate. You may not be able or willing to do so when the time comes and your student will not appreciate their adverse credit report and mounting debt they alone are responsible for.

Military Aid

For those who are called to serve in the military, significant educational benefits may be available following their service. Under certain circumstances some benefits may be available for spouses or children as well. Visit www.va.gov or www.nationalguard.com for more information, and carefully consider the requirements to qualify for education benefits. In addition, college credit may be available for training received while in the military.

State Aid

Many states also have free grant money for you to attend college. For example New York State has the Tuition Assistance Program (TAP). This grant could pay students more than $5,000 per year based on financial need and is available for full-time and part-time students. With rare exception, states will not allow state financial aid funds to be used at schools in other states. You should check with your appropriate state agency to see what may be available for the student and learn the criteria for each type of benefit. The agency website is always the best place to begin, but high school counselors and the college financial aid office should also have information.

Chapter 5
What Every Student and Parent Needs to Know about Student Loans

When I give my financial aid lectures, I spend the most time discussing the importance of understanding student loans, both for parents and students. Over the years, I have been asked more questions about this topic than any other. One of the most important facts that parents and students alike should know about loans is that loans are not free money like grants, and students and parents who borrow education loans need to pay these loans back. The nation's student loan debt burden now exceeds one trillion dollars, reportedly more than the nation's credit card debt (8)."

We have all seen the articles in papers and magazines on the increasing student loan debt and the effect the debt load has on students, their families, and institutions of higher learning. For the student, these loans are an awesome responsibility. Student loans are not subject to a credit check and are readily accessible at almost every college in America. This fact alone may put a careless student loan borrower in serious financial jeopardy.

The loan process

I will be discussing the many types of student loans available to students a little later in this chapter. However, before discussing the terms and conditions of those loans, it is import that you are aware of the process you will go through in order to obtain a student loan.

All federal student loans require a student to perform some type of loan counseling. Known as the "entrance counseling session", most schools ask students to go to the Department of Education's website, www.studentloans.gov, also available through the link found at www.direct.ed.gov.

Both websites are dedicated to the subject of federal student loans. For their first loan, students must complete this online tutorial that provides useful tips and tools to help students manage and develop a budget for their educational expenses and think about their borrowing. In addition, it will provide students with a full understanding of what student loans are and a full disclosure of their rights and responsibilities when borrowing student loans. Please remember that if the student plans to take out a student loan it is a requirement that they complete the FAFSA application first.

Once they complete their entrance interview it is now time for them to complete what is known as the electronic Master Promissory Note (MPN). This too can be completed at www.studentloans.gov or www.direct.ed.gov. The MPN is a legal document that explains the terms and conditions of the loan and commits the student to repay the loan and any interest and fees to the Department of Education when the time comes. To complete the MPN the student will need some pertinent information, which includes but is not limited to the following items:

- Student name
- Address

- Date of Birth
- Social Security Number
- Name and contact information of two references
- Signature

Once the student completes the MPN and signs it, they are promising the U.S. Department of Education they will pay the loan back. It is extremely important that the parents do not take it upon themselves to complete the entrance counseling and MPN steps for their student. First, it is against the law to do so. Second, the student must be fully aware they are taking out a loan that must be repaid, by them, which will show up on their credit report as well. Many students and parents have broken relationships because the parent, typically with good intentions, took out a loan without the student's knowledge or understanding.

After the student signs the MPN, the college will certify their loan via the federal government. The funds will then be sent electronically to the institution and will apply to the student's bill as early as ten days before or as late as thirty days after the first day of the enrollment period, depending on the school's loan disbursement policy.

Things students must consider before borrowing

Some thoughts have probably crossed your mind by now. What if the student can't pay their loans back after they graduate? What if they can't find a job? What if they didn't like the quality of their education? Regardless of what their situation is after they graduate, your child is required to pay their loans back.

Typically there is a 6-month deferment period that the government grants them once they either graduate, fall below 6 credit hours in their current program of study, or withdraw from college. This deferment period is designed to give students time to enroll in another program of study (which means the loan will go back into "in-school" deferment) or give the student enough time to find a job to start paying on their loan balances. Not paying on a student loan is not a wise option. As they will see, if the student fails to pay on a student loan there can be some very serious ramifications for them.

As a student loan borrower there are two different situations that can jeopardize their financial future. The first situation is known as delinquency. A student loan is considered delinquent if a payment has not been received the day after the payment due date. Just like car loans, home loans, or personal loans, student loans need to be paid on time in order to keep your student out of financial trouble.

Often, people take a lackadaisical approach to student loans, as they view them as unimportant when compared to mortgage loans, car loans, or any type of collateralized loan. People tend to pay for loans that they think are more important. When in financial trouble, borrowers tend to pay first on loans when they know that the items attached to them can be repossessed or foreclosed on. This is an unfortunate practice as student loans are different from most unsecured loans in many ways, as you will see.

The second situation that can occur on a student loan is known as default. Default occurs at 270 days of delinquency, or non-payment, on a student loan. This means that the government now deems the student's delinquent loan as bad debt and they will be subject to the following ramifications in an effort to collect their defaulted loan:

- Reported to Credit Bureaus
- Income tax refunds and other Federal payments withheld
- Wages can be garnished and lottery winnings withheld
- Professional license may not be renewed (such as Nursing or Cosmetologist)

- Not eligible for future Federal financial aid
- Not eligible for certain Federal benefits
- They will be responsible for all debt collection costs
- They will be sued for the balance they owe

Student borrowers should also know that student loans are exempt from bankruptcy, so if they cannot pay their student loans there is no protection for them under bankruptcy law.

> **Director's Tip:**
> Students never have to borrow the full amount of student loans offered. Loans can be reduced to just what a student needs and increased later if needed. Also, the full amount of the loan is not available up front, but usually split evenly between academic terms, a common misstep by students who expect the full amount will apply to their first bill.

My reasoning for discussing student loan default and delinquency first was not meant to scare you or prevent your student from borrowing student loans; it was meant to make sure they are educated and savvy borrowers. The grim reality is that most students will have to borrow a student loan at some point during their college education. Students must understand and recognize how student loans work and what pitfalls should be avoided, and must know the difference between different types of loans.

Types of loans

Now that you as a parent are aware of the great responsibilities your student will undertake when borrowing a student loan it is time to take a look at what types of loans are available for a student to borrow to help offset the cost of a college education. In a nutshell, there are five basic types of student loans available to a student and their families to offset the cost of school.

Perkins Loan

This low interest loan is granted to undergraduate or graduate students with exceptional need. Availability of this loan may be limited, and not all colleges participate in the Federal Perkins Loan Program. The criteria and maximum loan limit is up to $5,500 for an undergraduate or up to $8,000 for a graduate student, as determined by the policies of the school. The Perkins Loan program has a fixed 5% interest rate and has a separate entrance counseling and Promissory Note requirement. This program may not be available in the future.

Federal Direct Subsidized Loan

This loan is awarded to students with exceptional need. Freshman students could receive a loan amount up to $3,500, sophomores, $4,500 and juniors and seniors could receive up to $5,500 per year up to a maximum of $23,000 all years combined.

The term "subsidized" means that the interest on these student loans will be paid by the government while the borrower is in school at least half time. This historically low fixed interest rate is reset for new loans annually based on the prime interest rate, and can be found at www.studentloans.gov.

Federal Direct Subsidized loans have a six-month deferment period that begins after the student stops attending college, falls below half-time or graduates. This deferment period is to help a student prepare for repayment of their loans via giving the student some time to find a job or make arrangements to repay their loans.

It is important to understand that due to recent Department of Education changes students can only borrow a Federal Direct Subsidized for a maximum of a 150% of their time frame of study. In other words, for a student who attends a two year college pursuing a two year degree, that student can only receive up to three years of a subsidized loan. After the third year that student would no longer be able to borrow a subsided loan as long as they continue to attend a two-year institution or pursue a two-year program.

The same would be true for a four-year college; however the maximum time frame to receive a subsidized student loan would be 6 years. For one-year certificate programs the loss of subsidy would occur after a year and a half.

Federal Direct Unsubsidized Loan

This loan is not based on financial need; a dependent student can borrow up to $2,000 a year, more if they do not qualify for the full amount of subsidized loans. This amount may be increased by up to $4000 a year for independent students or for those students whose parents are denied a Parent PLUS loan. (If your Parent PLUS loan application was denied, the student should seek help from their college financial aid office if they want a loan increase.)

Unlike subsidized loans, interest on an unsubsidized loan accrues, or is added to the loan debt, immediately (visit www.studentloans.gov for current rates). Federal Direct Unsubsidized loans also have a six-month deferment period after the student stops attending college, falls below half time or graduates before repayment begins.

Parent PLUS loans

In order to qualify for a parent PLUS loan, you must be the legal parent of a dependent undergraduate student. You do not have to be the custodial parent nor the parent listed on the FAFSA to apply. Please note that a credit check is required on the parent for this type of loan. In order to receive this loan the parent must not have an adverse credit history, although requirements have been relaxed and an appeal process is in place, allowing parents to be approved often under somewhat adverse credit conditions.

The loan amount the parent requests may be reduced by the college based on the institution's cost of attendance minus any other aid the student is receiving. Parent PLUS loan interest rates and an application link can be found at www.studentloans.gov. Repayment of Parent PLUS loans begins in 60 days unless the parent chooses to defer their payment in sync with the student's loan deferment.

Funds from Plus loans can only be used for educational expenses, not the parent's own financial needs, and failure to stay current on these loans can prevent your student from receiving future aid. Parents, also, should be careful, borrowing only what is needed and what they can afford to pay back. It is not possible to transfer parent loan debt to the student, nor student debt to the parent, and this debt will show on the parent's credit report. Parents, if you cannot afford it, just say "no". You are under no obligation to go into debt for your child's education. Do not jeopardize your own financial security to do so, nor expect your student to repay your Plus loan after college.

If you simply must find more financial resources, consult your financial advisor before making decisions about funding your student's education by divesting other assets or taking out a PLUS loan.

Private or Alternative Loans

The term 'private' means that these loans come from private banks or lenders; not the government. You should also be aware that some colleges do not participate in private loan programs. Students can borrow up to the cost of attendance less any financial aid received. Any applicant for a private loan will be required to pass certain income criteria and a credit check. Private loans also may not have an interest rate cap, may have variable interest rates and a cosigner may be required.

Finally, when the student's repayment period begins, private loans cannot be consolidated with federal Direct loans into the same lump payment and do not have terms and conditions as favorable as federal Direct loans.

> **Director's Tip:**
> I would strongly suggest that students use private or alternative loans only as a last resort. All students qualify for Direct student loans, which generally have much better interest rates and terms than private loans, unless the student has poor academic standing, is enrolled less than 1/2 time or has borrowed the maximum possible in Direct student loans.

Watch Out for These Loan Pitfalls

My best advice to students and their families is to only borrow what you need for the current year - you will be offered additional loans every year you meet academic requirements, as long as you don't overborrow.

Although it may not be the most interesting reading in the world, it is a good idea for the student to read all parts of their loan agreement before they sign it. Be sure they understand the exact loan terms that they are agreeing to. SOME STUDENTS DON'T REALIZE LOANS NEED TO BE PAID BACK! Most terms of Federal Student loans require a ten-year repayment plan with a minimum $50 per month payment and favorable early payback options.

PARENTS: NEVER sign loan documents in the student's name or on their behalf. Not only is it fraudulent, your student may not find it easy to forgive you when they discover they have thousands of dollars in loans to repay.

There are programs through the military, the federal government and a variety of private and public organizations to pay student loans off as a benefit. Though this can be a great help, be careful – each of these offers comes with an obligation on the student's part, often to work or volunteer a certain number of years, and requires strict adherence to the rules. Above all, do not increase your borrowing unnecessarily just because there is a future promise from a third party to pay those loans off.

Many parents lived through a period when it was hard to be approved for a loan, and that fear sometimes leads them to encourage their student to load up on loans even if they don't need them, just in case they can't get loans later in life. Don't advise your student to take on a mountain of debt, just because it is "easy" money; they could quickly ruin their financial future. Students with high student loan debt often have great trouble after college being approved for a mortgage or car loan, or may have fewer career options due to their debt obligation. Teach them how to live like a student today so they don't have to live like one for the rest of their life, simply because they immersed themselves in a pile of debt from which there is no escape.

> ### Director's Tip:
> My simple rule of thumb when it comes to borrowing loans: if you don't have to borrow a student loan, then don't. If you do have to borrow a loan, be a savvy, educated loan borrower and borrow only the amount you need. Being educated and savvy means knowing exactly what borrowing a student loan entails and reading everything about your loan terms before taking out student loans.

Chapter 6
Budgeting and Building Positive Credit

It's almost impossible for a student to be able to make good borrowing decisions without some basic understanding of budgeting and their all-important credit history. Unfortunately, many students enter college already in debt, or having worked throughout high school with nothing to show for their hard work due to poor spending and saving habits.

Often, college is the first time students have to really think about having enough money to buy food or gas, keeping a checking account balanced or navigating their way through unscrupulous offers of credit from car lots, retailers, credit card companies and online financial predators anxious to get their private information.

Budgeting and Credit Cards

In order to understand the economics of education, one must understand what a budget is and, more importantly, how to live by one. Let's face it: we can't spend more money than we earn without getting into financial trouble. A budget, simply put, is living within your economic means. Your student must know the difference between a "want" and a "need". Your student may want a million dollar mansion and a Corvette, but what they really need is affordable housing and reliable transportation. Here are some interesting debt facts:

- The average household carried a balance of $15,355 on credit cards as of September 2015. (9)

- In 2015 Americans owed more than $712 billion on credit cards (9).

- Thanks to the Credit Card Act only 14% of freshman students have credit cards, yet freshmen carry the highest balances of all college students. (10)

Every parent should insist that their son or daughter create their own monthly budget program. There are many interactive programs available to students to accomplish this very task. One of my favorites is www.cashcourse.org. On sites such as CashCourse students can create their own monthly budget and find other useful financial information such as: understanding the financial aid process, what to look for in renting an apartment, understanding taxes and banking, and even how to talk to parents about money.

Whatever budgeting program your child will use, it is important that they track and categorize their monthly spending and income. In their budgets they should not only allow for fixed costs but should also plan for unexpected expenses.

> ## Case Study:
> ### What do minimum credit card payments cost?
> *Teach your student that they should never charge more in a month than they can repay within the month. Maintaining a credit card balance over time can cost them in the long run.*
>
> *This example illustrates how long it can take to pay off a $2000 balance on a credit card and how expensive it can be to only pay the minimum due.*
>
> $2,000 purchase on 15% interest card
> $30.00 per month minimum payment
>
> Time to pay off: 11 years and 8 months
> (with no additional purchases to card)
>
> Total repayment cost: $4,200
> (the $2,000 original purchase and $2,200 in interest)

A savvy student will always look for ways to cut expenses. Help your student reduce costs using some of the methods listed below:

1. Live with parents when possible instead of living on campus.

2. If you are not required to live on campus, see if there are less expensive housing units close to campus and consider sharing the cost with a roommate.

3. Eat at home or in the campus dining hall or learn to cook instead of eating out at restaurants.

4. Don't overspend on travel and entertainment.

5. Use the college computer lab instead of buying a computer.

6. Buy or rent used text books or e-books.

7. Buy used furniture.

8. Try to carpool.

9. Get a part-time job.

Getting a job serves two purposes: you can earn extra money, and you have less time to spend it. If you qualify for work study jobs on campus take advantage of this benefit as you will not have to travel back and forth to work.

Students should also get in the habit of maintaining files for their student loan documents and billing statements. This will help students stay informed on what they owe and help them track monthly payments.

> **Director's Tip:**
> Here's a simple truth: if your student does not have a job, they should not have a credit card, since they have no way to pay their bill. Students should absolutely not plan on using their financial aid to pay their credit card bill. Instead, they should deposit financial aid refunds in a savings account and draw out funds when needed, or save for future terms. College students don't like to think of themselves as vulnerable, but we know that they are susceptible to all sorts of temptations, including unethical people and companies trying to part them from their money.

Helping your student build positive credit

Many students are under the mistaken impression that taking out a student loan helps build a positive credit history. In truth, taking out loans hurts their credit until years later when they start to pay those loans back, and if they ever miss a payment or only pay the minimum, that debt will hurt their credit, not help it.

I recommend that each student have no more than one credit card if they want to build a positive credit history. However, because of the federal CARD Act of 2009, many students under age 21 will need a co-signer to qualify for their own credit card, often a parent. Remember that co-signing on your student's card also reflects on your credit. Students should pay cash when they can, and only charge items that they need. It is also important that students pay off their credit card balances every month and avoid late payments and fees.

The spending and borrowing habits your student establishes in college will greatly affect their lifestyle after college, including where they live, what they drive, their personal relationships, and their everyday financial options.

Helping your student avoid predatory creditors

Before you send your student off to college, arm them with some basic rules to live by:

1. Never sign anything at a car lot without an experienced and trusted advisor to help you negotiate and look for better offers or terms. That sweet ride may be tempting, but repairing your old car may make more sense right now.

2. Never give verbal agreement to anything nor any private information over the phone. Don't trust anyone who asks you for that information.

3. Shred unwanted credit applications and monitor your credit throughout the year for identity theft.

4. Learn how to balance your checking account and monitor it at least weekly for unauthorized debits.

5. Stay away from revolving accounts offered by retailers. They hurt your credit and lead to unnecessary spending.

6. Put your financial aid refund checks in a safe place and draw out funds when educational expenses come up.

> **Director's Tip:**
>
> Let's be honest. You as a parent may not have had the best financial training and may have made your own share of precarious financial choices. Most of us have learned about handling money the hard way, and our children have observed our money habits all their lives. They may be skeptical about listening to our advice.
>
> If you aren't qualified to give your student the best financial advice, or if they simply won't listen to you, find someone they respect who is wise with money and enlist their help. Don't let your pride or your own family's financial legacy set your student up for financial instability.
>
> By the same token, it is never too late for you to learn, start making wise decisions, and prepare your student for college with common sense and good information about paying for college.

Chapter 7
Top Ten Most Costly Parent Mistakes

With all good intention, sometimes parents make very costly mistakes when it comes to helping their child pay for college. Here are the most common or most expensive mistakes every financial aid office has seen parents make:

1. **Having the student move out**
   Don't make plans for that extra room just yet – living on their own does not mean your information will not be required on the FAFSA, and living at home is one of the easiest ways to trim college costs. In fact, make sure your student has a quiet place to study at home, preferably with stable Internet access.

2. **Emancipating the student**
   Some divorce decrees stipulate the student will be 'emancipated'

on their 18th birthday. This does not mean they can answer "yes" to the emancipation question on the FAFSA. Parent information is still required. Once a student reaches the age of majority in their state, usually age 18, they are no longer considered a minor; emancipation at this point is expensive and useless as far as financial aid is concerned.

3. **Using the wrong parent(s) on the FAFSA**

   Students do not get to choose which parent to use on the FAFSA, in cases where the parents are divorced, separated or remarried. Here are the rules:

   - The student always uses the parent with whom they live or stayed with the most when they last lived with a parent. If that parent is remarried, the spouse's information is included, even if they have a pre-nuptial agreement absolving the new spouse from children's education expenses.*

   - If the student's parents, biological or adoptive, are not married but live together, both parents must be on the FAFSA.

   - If the parent's marriage is legal anywhere in the world, both people must be included on the FAFSA.

   - If the parents split after the student moved out, the student uses the parent that most recently provided the highest amount of support.

   Correcting this type of error after the fact is often difficult and costly, forcing the student to repay funds they have received or find ways to cover an unexpected bill late in the academic term.

*Even though many parents claim to have a 50/50 shared custody agreement, financial aid officers will tell you there is no such thing as a 50/50 split; someone always pays more, either by carrying the insurance or in some other way. The student generally knows who this is.

4. **Miscounting the number of household members or number in college**

   Parents often don't realize they can include older children not living at home in the household number on the FAFSA, provided that sibling would have to include the same parent information on their FAFSA, should they decide to go to college. You can also include grandparents who have moved in, or anyone, regardless of age, relative or not, living on your property, as long as you are providing more than 50% of their support.

   The number in the household going to college can also be confusing. Parents cannot be counted in this number, though any of the other household members can, even if they do not live at home. The student is always counted in the household, even if he doesn't live at home. Review the following case study.

5. **Cashing out retirement**

   Many parents are tempted to cash out their retirement to pay for "Junior's" college. Not only will you be required to pay a hefty tax on that early cash-out, but you are putting your future financial stability in jeopardy, which will eventually come back to burden your children. Avoid this expensive option at all costs.

6. **Refusing to provide information on the FAFSA**

   Sometimes parents refuse to provide information on the FAFSA, perhaps because 1) they don't trust the government or the school, 2) they don't understand why it is required, 3) they are afraid their tax returns will be audited, 4) they do not want their student to know what they earn or are not getting along with them, or 5) the parent does not have a legal Social Security number.

   The truth is, the Department of Education never shares information with the IRS, and only receives information from the IRS if the parent or student give permission. FAFSA compliance does not trigger tax return audits, and parents without Social Security numbers can enter all zeros in place of this number without fear.

If parents refuse to help with the FAFSA the student is ineligible for any aid and can only get a loan if the parent signs a separate letter of refusal. The best way to address these concerns is to make an appointment to visit the financial aid officer at your college.

> ### *Case Study: Who's in the Household?*
>
> *Ramone lives at home with his parents, grandparents, his 27-year-old sister Celia and her baby, and his Aunt Gloria, all of whom are supported by his father and mother. He has an older brother, Enrique, age 23, who lives on his own, is not married or in the military and has no children, and another sister, Julia, age 28, who also lives on her own.*
>
> *Both of his sisters and his mother are also enrolled in college, working toward their own degrees.*
>
> *Ramone's household includes 9 people (Ramone, his two parents, his two grandparents, his aunt, his sister Celia and her child, and his brother, Enrique).*
>
> *Two members are counted as "in college" on the FAFSA (Ramone and Celia). Julia is not in the household or number in college because she is over 24 and not living at home. Parents cannot be included in the number in college.*

7. Misstating assets on the FAFSA

If parents are required to enter a value for their assets on the FAFSA, they should not include their family home and personal belongings or cars. They should not include any retirement assets such as 401K or IRA accounts or other retirement savings.

Parents living on and working a family farm should not include the value of this farm. Small business owners with less than 100 employees should not include the value of their business assets.

Do you own a second home? The liquidation value of that property should be included. Did you cash out a 401K? It will show on your tax return as taxable income – don't add it to this question as well. Did you convert a traditional retirement IRA to a Roth IRA? This will be included in your Adjusted Gross Income on the FAFSA, but you can file a special circumstance appeal with the office of financial aid to have it removed.

> **Director's Tip:**
> Never deliberately enter false information on the FAFSA, even if a professional recommends it. Bad advice comes from everywhere, but costs for this error could be high.
>
> The U.S. Department of Education compares FAFSA data year to year and financial aid professionals are required to audit discrepancies and correct or cancel aid if needed, as well as report known fraud.
>
> The statement both parent and student agree to at the end of the FAFSA application states "If you purposely give false or misleading information, you may be fined up to $20,000, sent to prison, or both."

8. **Not involving the student in the financial process**
   When parents "take care" of their adult children by completing and signing legal documents on their behalf as they have been in the habit of doing through the high school years, the student never learns to watch for important messages and deadlines, and often does not realize they have a bill to pay or a loan taken out in their name. Imagine how you would feel if your student

applied for a parent loan in your name! Not only is this illegal, it can seriously harm your relationship. Also, parents often misenter their student's email or use their own emails when filling out forms for their children and then forget to check the messages that come to them, or don't notice them in their junk mail folder.

Remember, parents don't receive important school messages and cannot call in for information due to FERPA laws (Family Education Right to Privacy Act); consequently, bills go unpaid, fees mount and students not in the habit of following up lose out.

9. **Expecting the student to work too many hours**
Parents, often anxious to see their children take on adult responsibility, sometimes do not appreciate the work required to succeed in college, particularly if the parent has never attended, and expect their student to work whenever they are not in class. A little work is good – a lot of work can cause a student to fail or have to repeat expensive classes. For every one credit hour taken, a student should reserve three hours each week to complete class assignments and study. A student attending 15 hours will need 45 hours a week or more for class work.

Many parents remember working and going to school full-time and believe they are encouraging a strong work ethic by requiring or pressing their students to do the same. Like it or not, your student came from a different generation, was educated in a different environment and works under different expectations than you experienced. Also, the demands of college are vastly different than they were a generation ago. Your student may also have learning disabilities you are not aware of. Before demanding a schedule that may be setting your student up to fail, take the time to learn about these issues.

Talk to your student well ahead of time about your worries and the limits of your ability to support them. Help them set reasonable work hours with plenty of schedule gaps for unexpected situations, and if they can't work as much, they may need a little cash now and then. Are they living at home while going to school? You have a right to expect them to follow certain rules and help out, but they need a quiet place to study and a little freedom as well. Talking through and establishing boundaries and expectations ahead of time helps everyone make good decisions.

10. Letting the student miss important deadlines

Sometimes parents are too "hands-off" when it comes to financial aid. Many students are still learning to take care of things themselves that their parent has always done for them.

Meeting deadlines may be the one area parents should be hypervigilant about. Don't let your students miss important deadlines. Especially for students who are fully Pell-eligible, missing a state deadline could easily mean the difference between having their entire bill covered and having a large bill to worry about. Missing a scholarship deadline could cost ongoing benefits as renewable scholarships go to other students. This is too high a price to pay for teaching your child responsibility.

In some states the FAFSA must be submitted as early as October 1 to qualify for state aid. Remember, if you filed a tax return extension, you don't need to have taxes complete to file the FAFSA. Parents and students can file using estimates and use the FAFSA tax return import feature a couple weeks after tax returns are filed. However, you will likely not receive financial aid until those returns are filed and the FAFSA updated, so file your tax return as quickly as possible. Most students need parents' personal and income information as well as a parent's electronic signature on their FAFSA.

Students should start working on scholarship applications early, well before the time comes to file the FAFSA, and often must do so every year. Scholarship deadlines are posted on the school or organization website or on the actual application.

In addition, your school may have priority deadlines for completing any extra paperwork that is required to receive financial aid. Often those papers require parent information and a signature. Miss those deadlines and your child may at minimum incur late fees; in a worst-case scenario they may forfeit their aid for the first academic period, be unable to get needed books in time to do well in their classes, and be unable to register for the following session or transfer because of their unpaid bill.

Chapter 8
Avoiding Scholarship Pitfalls

Applying for scholarships can be a slippery slope for many first time college students. The biggest myth about scholarships is that they are only available for the smartest students with the highest grades. The truth is, there are scholarships for all types of students. The key to getting scholarship money is : GET ORGANIZED and START EARLY.

First and foremost, *parents should not complete any part of the scholarship process for the student.* **This entire chapter, then, is addressed directly to the student.** Read and talk about it together:

Before you apply for scholarships

1. **Register for and take your first college entrance exam.** SAT (The Scholastic Aptitude Test) and ACT (American College Testing) are two college entrance exams that bring plenty of anxiety to parents and students. These exams test the student's knowledge, skill and understanding on subjects that are emphasized in high school, including Language, Writing, Reading, and Math.

   According to *collegeboard.org*, the website where students register to take the SAT and complete the CSS/Financial Aid PROFILE application, at least half of all students take the SAT twice – in the spring of their junior year and again the following fall of their senior year. For schools requiring the ACT test, students can register at *actstudent.org*. Registration ends at least a month before the test date, and seats are limited. Tests are only offered a few times a year and charge a registration fee. Tests last 3-4 hours, so eat a good breakfast that morning and make sure you print and bring your ticket along with your photo ID, sharp pencils with erasers, and the right kind of calculator, if permitted. No ticket and ID, no admission, no exceptions.

> **Director's Tip:**
> These tests cost over $50 each time they are taken, more if you register late; however, fee waivers are available for both tests through your high school guidance counselor. Home-schooled students must also find a high school counselor for fee waivers. Criteria for fee waivers are on their websites, but generally if the student receives any low-income benefits or free/reduced price lunch they will probably qualify. Special accommodations are also available for students with disabilities.

2. **Pick your top 5.** No later than the summer before your senior year, narrow your college choices down to your top three to five schools and find out their deadlines for admission application and scholarship application, as well as which college entrance exam they require. Some deadlines may be as early as a year ahead.

3. **Narrow down your scholarship choices.** For each of your top 5, list the scholarships you want to try for and know their requirements. Often, one application covers a long list of scholarships. Many schools require the CSS/Financial Aid PROFILE application completed online at www.collegeboard.org. This step

may seem tedious, but it will help you avoid becoming overwhelmed by the scholarship process.

4. **Apply for admission.** You can apply for admission to more than one school at a time, and should apply at each of your top three to five choices. Applying for scholarships at a school you haven't yet applied for admission to is a waste of time. No school will give you money if you have not applied for admission yet, and some schools block access to their scholarship application without a valid college-issued student ID number.

Even if a school asks for an early commitment or pledge to attend, even if you accept a scholarship, you are not legally obligated to attend that school. You can change your mind right up to the first day of class - **unless you legally signed a letter of intent (13)** or other document. DO NOT SIGN DOCUMENTS UNTIL YOU HAVE READ THEM THOROUGHLY AND UNDERSTAND YOUR OBLIGATIONS. Once you do make a decision, though, have the courtesy to notify the other schools.

> **Director's Tip:**
> NCAA rules are tight and very specific. Athletes must protect themselves by knowing NCAA rules, not only so they don't accidentally break a rule, but so they are not taken advantage of by schools, recruiters and coaches anxious to sign them. Before you sign a letter of intent, make sure you have read and understand every word. Visit ncaa.org and nationalletter.org. Highly recruited athletes in particular may benefit from enlisting a trusted attorney to help sort out the fine print. .

5. **Submit your SAT or ACT college entrance exam test scores before scholarship deadlines.** Because college entrance tests can be taken multiple times, students sometimes fail to send their scores to their colleges of choice until they've had

a chance to improve them. However, if you want to be in the running for scholarships that look at these test results, scores must be sent to the schools prior to the scholarship deadline. You don't have to send scores or choose which colleges they go to when you take the test, but forgetting to go back to the website and send your scores by those deadlines could cost you thousands in scholarship money. You can retake both the SAT and ACT and send updated test scores in as well, even if it's after a scholarship or admission deadline. Schools always use the best of each category to give you the highest total score possible.

Types of scholarships

Academic Scholarships- Yes, these are the scholarships that everyone hears about that are awarded to the brightest students with the highest GPA's (Grade Point Average) or who have scored the highest on some type of academic achievement test. These scholarship dollars are limited and highly competitive. At many schools, students with 3.8 GPA still do not qualify for scholarship. Often, weighted GPA's also are not taken into consideration for scholarships, leaving students who worked hard in high school taking challenging college-level coursework feeling disillusioned. It's safe to say that studying hard in high school to earn a high GPA has benefits more important than earning college scholarships. The student is far more prepared to succeed in college and may even have earned valuable college credit. Considering the high cost of going to college, every credit should be thought of as a college scholarship the student earned while in high school.

That said, colleges hope to attract the most sought-after students and know it is a competitive environment. Many colleges have a separate pocket of endowed scholarships they may offer to the best and brightest students or the top performers in athletics or the arts. If you are the parent of one of these students, colleges may have already offered attractive financial aid packages to your student. In many cases you will be able to compare offers they have received and use those offers as a negotiation instrument to help secure a better financial aid package. Often you are working with a recruiter who may not even be an employee of the university. Be wise and fact-check everything.

Athletic Scholarships- These are a great source of funding for college for the exceptional athlete who has excelled in his or her sport, but athletic scholarships are extremely competitive. The NCAA reports that only about 2% of high school athletes receive even a small athletic scholarship. For Division I schools, only 1% of the more than seven million high school athletes nationwide get a full ride scholarship[12]. Remember that even with a generous athletic scholarship you may not be able to afford the school, and these scholarships are easily lost due to injury, marginal athletic OR academic performance. In the end, parents and students should keep first things first; the student should walk away with an education. 98% of all student athletes will NOT 'go pro' but WILL depend on their education for their life and work after college [12]. Help your child choose the school for its academics and their career path first. This is FAR more important than the short-term pride of being in a particular athletic program or being able to continue playing sports in college.

> **Director's Tip**
> Be cautious when recruiters or coaches make bold promises of scholarships. They may not be completely trustworthy. Be sure you understand when the scholarship will be paid, under what terms it renews, what the school's costs are and, above all, get it all in writing. Many capable athletes and other high-achieving students and their families have been left high and dry by unscrupulous recruiters or schools who entice them with promises they can't keep.

Special skill/interest Scholarships- Many future college students may have a hobby or special skill that they often don't think about when searching for scholarships. For example your son or daughter may excel in theater or may be on his way to being the greatest guitarist since Jimmy Hendrix. If so keep in mind that there are many colleges that offer theater, fine arts or music scholarships. In addition, colleges offer Science, Technology, Engineering, and Mathematics (STEM incentive scholarships) which often cover an associates or bachelor's degree program in one of these areas of study. So, don't discount that robot project Junior has been working on in the basement, as it could lead to some serious cash for college.

Equal Opportunity Scholarships- There are also many scholarships that benefit minority groups. If you belong to a minority group of any kind you should consult your group's website or regional office to see what scholarships may be available. For example, many Native Americans seek out the help of their tribal councils on their reservations to see what types of Native American scholarships may be available. The foundation of your school of choice may also have scholarships geared toward particular under-represented groups. Search their website for details on how to apply. Is your student a female? In recent years many scholarships have been created for women to attend college in an effort to encourage women to pursue careers in fields that have been dominated by men for many years, particularly STEM fields, and to level enrollment in those majors in higher education.

Community Service Scholarships- Often this type of scholarship is overlooked or forgotten about. Many organizations such as the Knights of Columbus or Rotary Club encourage young men and women to volunteer their time for the purposes of helping out in the community in which they live. Not only does this type of activity prepare future college students with valuable life and job experience, many organizations will reward these volunteers with scholarships to attend local colleges. I personally believe that volunteering in your community is very important as many colleges that offer scholarships give extra scoring points for applications that include community service. Volunteering demonstrates a character trait that scholarship donors are looking for, and educators know students who volunteer are better equipped to choose a major they will be happy with and are more likely to succeed in college.

Employer scholarships- Many companies who want to improve skill sets of their workers or retain quality employees may offer scholarships, not for just their employees, but for their spouses and children as well. Parents, students and spouses should check with their employer's Human Resource department to see what may be available to help offset the cost of a college education.

Online Scholarships- There are many online scholarships that offer a plethora of scholarships for every type of college student imaginable. Fastweb.com is an example of an on line scholarship site. Searching for an online scholarship can be very time consuming, however it can also be rewarding. I always tell students to be very careful when surfing the internet for scholarships. Do your due diligence and make sure scholarship websites are legitimate. You should never pay fees to any company or organization to apply for or help you find a scholarship. Beware of claims that promise scholarship dollars. If your time is limited, focus on local and school scholarships where competition is lower.

When all is said and done, the best place for the high school senior and junior to start looking for scholarships is right in their own high school guidance office. Guidance counselors are seasoned professionals that are more than happy to assist students with their scholarship hunt. Guidance counselors work with many colleges both in and out of state. Students must get to know their high school guidance counselors and the services they provide.

The Scholarship Application Process

Deadlines- Please keep in mind that all colleges have scholarship filing deadlines. Many high school students wait until the last minute to apply for scholarships only to be disappointed that they missed the application cutoff point. These deadlines are often months in advance of the particular semester you are applying for. For example the fall semester deadline for scholarships may close as early as a year prior to the fall semester. Most high school seniors should have a good idea where they want to attend college, therefore it is important that you contact or check the website of the college's foundation or scholarship offices that are on your list to find out what scholarships those institutions offer and when the deadlines are for those scholarships.

Even if your student has a 4.0 GPA, a year's worth of college credit and many years of volunteer experience, if they walk into the financial aid or foundation office the summer before classes are to begin looking for scholarships, they will be disappointed. All scholarships will have already been awarded to students who met the deadlines. There is no pocket of money saved for procrastinators.

Essays- Most scholarships offered by colleges or community foundations require some type of essay to be written. I have experienced firsthand that $1000's in scholarship funds sometimes remain on the table because students do not want to spend the time or put forth the effort to write a simple essay. That's a shame, however this means that , if you are willing to put a little work into applying for a scholarship, it could mean free money for you. Let's face it, even if you are awarded a few $250 scholarships it adds up and is well worth your time to apply.

Always have another party read your scholarship essay. I have seen many essays disqualified for simple grammatical or spelling errors. Also, as obvious as it may sound, do not write like you text. In most cases professionals in your community make up a panel that review essays and before scholarship applications get to these individuals they are carefully screened to make sure that they are error-free and within the word limit. Many college scholarship offices offer free scholarship writing workshops that are open to the public; it is a good idea for you to take advantage of these for help with your essay. There are lots of great resources about writing essays, but other than writing a clean, error-free essay, the best advice I can give is to always tell the truth. Be open about your life experiences, and be yourself.

Reference Letters- Many scholarships are won or lost based on the contents of the reference letter. Scholarship committees can easily spot letters that are ingenuous, rushed, generic, even fake, and disregard letters that don't address their key criteria. Pick your references thoughtfully; teachers, advisors, mentors, bosses, civic leaders, clergy members and coaches can all be good sources of references. Students should avoid asking a relative or peer to be a reference. Make sure you choose a reference who can attest to your abilities for the specific scholarship that you are applying for. Once you have made a decision on what scholarships you want to apply for, meet with your references as early as possible to discuss the scholarships and what you are looking for in their reference letters. Writing a meaningful reference letter is hard and time-consuming, so approach your references with gratitude and respect. By giving your references plenty of advanced time they will be able to provide a more professional and well thought-out reference letter.

Some schools require reference letters to be submitted electronically, directly from the reference. Be sure you have given your reference everything they need to mail, email or upload their letter, including a pre-addressed, stamped envelope, and, if necessary, send a gentle reminder before the deadline if the school hasn't gotten their response yet. Also don't forget to drop your reference a note after their letter is submitted, thanking them for their time and effort.

I got a scholarship! Now what?

Compare offers-when "Bigger" isn't "Better" - Should you always go with the school offering the biggest scholarship? No. Some schools offer "scholarships" that are awarded to almost everyone to get the student in the door the first year. Compare scholarships and other aid to tuition and housing costs – the highest scholarship isn't necessarily the best offer to take. Read the details – the total amount offered may sound like a huge scholarship but the details may include loans also. Look at costs over four or five years. If the scholarship isn't renewable you may find yourself transferring to a less expensive college by your second year.

Use the Net Price Calculator - Many colleges are now required by law to post a mechanism online known as a Net Price Calculator that students can use to estimate their "net price" to attend college. Net price in a nutshell is the difference between sticker price to attend the college minus any grants and scholarships for which a students may be eligible for. Sticker price includes tuition, fees, room and board, books, supplies, transportation and school related expenses. Net price calculators are ONLY ESTIMATES, and should not be taken as gospel. Many net price calculators use one to two year-old data when calculating the net price. ALWAYS compare net prices between schools to know the true value of your scholarships, and be sure the estimates are accurate. If you have any questions at contact the bursar or financial aid offices of the college.

Accept your scholarships - Don't lose the money because you never officially accepted it. Follow the acceptance process carefully. Did you receive a scholarship from a source outside of the school such as a civic organization or community foundation? Make sure they have what they need to send the money to your school of choice, such as proof of enrollment, or your school's name and address. Send a hand-written thank you note directly to the donor of every scholarship you receive.

Chapter 9
Before Day One

Your student made the big decision about where they will go to college. They applied for admission and were accepted, they received their financial aid award notification and a scholarship or two as well. Time to relax, right? Wrong! There still remains a few items that they must do, any many expensive mistakes to make.

Pre-college requirements -It is very important that your child remains engaged with the college he or she will be attending. Most information will be on the school website and should be included in the admissions letter as well. READ EVERYTHING. In some cases your child may be required to take a placement test prior to enrollment or attending orientation, so you should learn when these exams are held and make sure that your child is on the testing schedule for an appointment. You should also inquire about when your child needs to register for classes and when new student orientation will occur. Whether your child will be living on campus or in nearby housing you will need to insure that your child has the proper living arrangements well ahead of time, which may require deposits and contracts. Remember, the early bird gets the worm. Procrastination means classes fill up, housing fills up, and chances for a smooth start dry up.

Early opportunity either for remedial classes or jumpstart college success programs usually happen in the summer, but registration for these programs will be the spring before. Hiring for jobs both off and on-campus also often happens before the first day of class, in late summer.

Where's the scholarship? Every year some students are shocked to find their promised scholarship money has been reduced or cancelled. If your student was expecting a scholarship and hasn't received it, or the amount of their award package on the award letter has changed, they need to contact the financial aid or scholarship offices to inquire why this change has occurred. Reasons for changes can range from an error, not registering for the proper classes or required number of credit hours, to the scholarship being rescinded. They may, in some cases, receive a revised award letter requiring them to turn in more information in order for their aid package to be complete. Whatever the reason for the discrepancy it is up to them to be diligent in following up with the proper offices on campus.

Know the rules - Please keep in mind that scholarships may affect other student aid. All aid added together can't be more than the cost of attendance at the college, and if scholarships are required by the donor to only pay for certain tuition or fees, other "tuition-specific" aid must be reduced. The rules about "who pays first" are set in stone by federal and state regulation, so you won't be able to argue this point. If your student was awarded a scholarship and will also be receiving additional financial aid awards or grants, let the financial aid office know as soon as possible so that they can adjust their aid if necessary and give a more accurate financial aid summary. Also, the scholarship may be split between terms; know the cost per term and the scholarships and other aid available per term to cover those costs, or you may be caught short.

Prepare for pre-college costs. The only thing more expensive than the last semester of high school is the month before college. Books, supplies, technology, clothes, car purchase or repair, and dorm room bling are expenses that fall before classes start and can quickly eat through your wallet. Extra financial aid funds will not be available until either just before or just after the start of classes. All those graduation checks your student received will come in handy now.

Grandparents also can be another source of funding. In my years in financial aid I have met with many grandparents that were willing to help pay for the grandchild's education, and these pre-college expenses may be a fun way for them to contribute. If there is a grandparent in the family willing and able to help, you should include them in your college cost discussions. You may be pleasantly surprised that they are more than willing to help out with the ever-rising cost of going to college.

Chapter 10

After Day One

Getting through the first billing cycle of the first year can be intimidating. Unfortunately, your involvement doesn't stop there. The FAFSA must be filed every year, as do scholarship applications, which means more deadlines. Don't let your student miss these deadlines!

Students can lose their right to receive aid the following year if they don't perform well academically in Year 1, so your job as a parent is to watch for signs the student is struggling, and do what you can to support them early, before they get too far behind. On the flip side, their scholarships may be renewable. If so, help them know what it takes to meet the requirements for renewal every year. It's a lot easier to keep money than replace it.

Often, students sign up for 'extra' classes, thinking they will drop one or two if they don't like the course or the professor. If they drop courses after the Registrar's "Drop/Add" period, a date you should find on their website, the student will have to pay for part of the course, will have a "W" on their academic record and may lose financial aid. Aid is always reviewed after this 'Drop/Add" period and may be either raised or lowered. Often, financial aid refunds are not sent until Week 2 for this reason, or students have to repay aid that has been adjusted or cover it with loans.

Did your student get a financial aid refund? If so they will be tempted to blow it on things they don't need or are not for their education. Refunds should be put in the bank and saved to cover education expenses that happen mid-term, buy books for the next term, pay back aid that was adjusted, or saved for future terms or possibly future study abroad or field experience classes that have extra costs. Can they use this money to pay for living expenses while in school? Yes. Can they use it for spring break? No.

Why do I owe money? Students who panic and drop classes mid-semester, or sign up for classes but never attend, or stop attending at some point may find themselves owing financial aid money back to the school before they can enroll for the next round of classes. Financial aid rules require schools to adjust aid during and after the term based on the student's actual attendance and enrollment through specific dates in the term. If a professor fails a student because they stopped attending or perhaps never attended, expect the student to lose aid for that term; sometimes $1000's of dollars must be cancelled, creating a large bill the student must pay back. Students should keep their class notes at least a year in case they have to prove they were in class.

Housing rules often also require full-time enrollment; if a school determines a student dropped or never attended a full-time schedule they could be kicked out of student housing. Make sure they know this.

College is hard. Teach your student to get help and advice from their school professionals early; their financial aid and academic advisors, professors, and the many support systems available at every school are there to help them succeed. Remember, due to FERPA privacy laws, if your student does run into such issues, you will not be successful calling to find out why they are not registered, or why they have a bill the following year.

For this reason, be sure to keep the lines of communication open. If they are struggling and feel they cannot talk to you honestly about it, their problems could easily snowball out of control. If your student has an emergency situation; an illness, accident, or personal tragedy, help them talk directly with professors, advisors, financial aid, the bursar's office and housing to keep such unexpected events from ruining their academic career. Every school should have options for appeal and extra help for such situations. However, your student is now an adult and must learn, as you did, how to push through difficult situations. A bad break-up or parents going through a divorce can send a student into a tailspin, but will not be grounds for an appeal, and missing a week or two of class as a result could have devastating results.

Adult on board! On this same subject, your student may very well be testing the freedoms of their new-found adulthood, and the college environment can offer many opportunities that make most parents shudder. The morals you instilled in them at an early age are still in there, so don't panic. You cannot control your adult student, nor protect them, but you can make sure they are well-informed and know how to be safe and smart about exercising their freedom. Overcome your discomfort and talk frankly with your student.

Is your student living at home? Your support might mean encouraging the student to cut back hours at work, reducing their home responsibilities, helping them eat healthy meals, helping with extra costs for tutors, getting medical help when needed, helping with transportation issues or laundry; in short, the same things you did for them when they were in high school. Only, this time they may be a lot more appreciative – as long as you have learned the art of parenting your adult child from a bit more distance, a skill that requires patience and practice.

With a little awareness and planning and your invaluable help, your student will have the best opportunity for success in their college endeavor and you, the all-important parent, will have survived your first adventure in the world of higher education and financial aid!

Endnotes

1. Alboher, M. "When It Comes to Careers, Change Is a Constant", The New York Times, May 1, 2007 edition (http://www.nytimes.com/2007/05/01/business/smallbusiness/01webcareers.html?_r=1&#)

2. "When Your College Student Changes Majors", College Parents of America blog, November 27, 2010 (http://www.collegeparents.org/blog/2010/11/27/when-your-college-student-changes-majors)

3. "Funding Your Education", The Guide to Federal Student Aid, U.S. Department of Education Office of Federal Student Aid (https://studentaid.ed.gov/sites/default/files/funding-your-education.pdf).

4. "Free Application for Federal Student Aid", U.S. Department of Education Office of Federal Student Aid (https://fafsa.ed.gov/options.htm)

5. "Funding Your Education", The Guide to Federal Student Aid, U.S. Department of Education Office of Federal Student Aid (https://studentaid.ed.gov/sites/default/files/funding-your-education.pdf)

6. "The SmartStudent Guide to Financial Aid", FinAid Page, LLC (http://www.finaid.org/)

7. Smith, J. Y. "Former R.I. Senator Claiborne Pell, 90; Sponsored Grant Program", Washington Post, January 2, 2009 (http://www.washingtonpost.com/wp-dyn/content/article/2009/01/01/AR2009010101521.html)

8. "Student Loan Debt Exceeds One Trillion Dollars", NPR "All Things Considered", April 24, 2012, Mark Kantrowitz interview by Melissa Block (http://www.npr.org/2012/04/24/151305380/student-loan-debt-exceeds-one-trillion-dollars)

9. http://www.nerdwallet.com/blog/credit-card-data/average-credit-card-debt-household/

10. "Money Essentials", http://money.cnn.com/magazines/money-mag/money101/

11. Larkin, Karen Y. "Average Credit Card Debt for a College Student", http://creditcards.lovetoknow.com/Average_Credit_Card_Debt_for_a_College_Student

12. NCAA Recruiting Fact Sheet, www.ncaa.org

13. National Letter of Intent, www.nationalletter.org

Additional Resources

U.S. Department of Education "The Guide to Federal Student Aid - Funding Your Education" Washington D.C. 2014, https://studentaid.ed.gov/resources

New York State Higher Education Services Corporation (HESC), "Financial Aid Nights" Albany, New York 12246. http://www.hesc.ny.gov/partner-access/high-school-counselors/financial-aid-nights.html

SUNY Smart Track "Empowered Financial Planning https://fa.financialavenue.org/suny-home/

Radio/Podcast interview with Chavon Tingle, Empire Radio, 12/27/2015 http://floempireradio.com/classactradioshowpodcast/